THE LIFE OF FIVE HOLY ABBOTS

THE LIFE OF FIVE HOLY ABBOTS

ST. BEDE THE VENERABLE

Copyright 2025 by Dalcassian Press

All rights reserved. No part of this book may be reproduced in any manner whatsoever without written permission except in the case of brief quotations embodied in critical articles and reviews.

No part of this publication may be reproduced, distributed, or transmitted in any form or by any means, including photocopying, recording, or other electronic or mechanical methods, without the prior written permission of the publisher, except in the case of brief quotations embodied in critical reviews and certain other non-commercial uses permitted by copyright law. For permission request, write to Dalcassian Press at admin@thescriptoriumproject.com

Translator: Curtin, D.P. (1985-)

ISBN: 979-8-3482-6679-0(Paperback)
ISBN: 979-8-3482-6680-6 (eBook)
Library of Congress Control Number:

Printed by Ingram Content Group, 1 Ingram Blvd, La Vergne, Tennessee
First Printing 2025, Dalcassian Press, Wilmington, DE

This work is part of a series produced in association with the Scriptorium Project and its community of scholars and translators.
Please visit our website at: www.thescriptoriumproject.com

1

Book One

The religious servant of Christ, a bishop named Benedict, inspired by heavenly grace, built a monastery in honor of the most blessed prince of the apostles, Peter, near the mouth of the river Wiri to the north, with the venerable and most pious king of that people, Ecgfrith, aiding him and granting the land; and he diligently governed the same monastery for sixteen years, amid countless labors of journeys and infirmities, with the same religious zeal with which he had built it. Who, to use the words of blessed Pope Gregory, which glorify the life of this abbot of his, was a man of venerable life, both by grace and by name Benedict, bearing a heart of old age from the very time of his youth, indeed passing through life with morals, gave his mind to no pleasure. Born of noble lineage of the Angles, but with no lesser nobility of spirit, always aspiring to earn the company of angels. Finally, when he was a minister of King Oswiu and was receiving the possession of land appropriate to his rank, at about twenty-five years of age he despised the fleeting possession in order to acquire the eternal; he disregarded military service with its corruptible earthly rewards, in order to serve the true King and merit to possess a kingdom in the heavenly city; he left home, relatives, and country for Christ and for the Gospel, so that he might receive a hundredfold and possess eternal life; he rejected the service of carnal marriage, so that he might be able to follow the Lamb, pure in the glory of virginity in the heavenly kingdoms; he refused to beget mortal children in the flesh, being predestined by Christ to raise spiritual sons for Him in the eternal life through heavenly teaching.

Therefore, having left his homeland, he went to Rome, where he had always been accustomed to ardently desire the blessed apostles, and he took care to visit and venerate the places of their bodies. Soon returning to his homeland, he did not cease to love, venerate, and preach with all his might the ecclesiastical life institutions he had seen. At that time, Alchfrith, the son of the aforementioned King Oswiu, also intending to come to Rome to venerate the thresholds of the apostles, took him as a companion for the journey. When his father recalled him from the intention of the journey and urged him to remain in his homeland and kingdom, nonetheless he, as a youth of good character, immediately fulfilled his purpose and hastened to Rome, at the time of blessed Pope Vitalian; and having drunk in the sweet knowledge of salvation as before, after a few months departing from there to the island of Lérins, he entrusted himself to the community of monks there, received the tonsure, and diligently observed the regular monastic discipline marked by his vow; where, having been instructed for two years in the suitable doctrine of monastic life, he was again overcome by the love of blessed Peter, the prince of the apostles, and decided to return to his sacred city.

Not long after, having arrived by merchant ship, he satisfied his desire. At that time, King Ecgberht of the Kentish sent from Britain a chosen man named Vighard to the office of bishop, who had been sufficiently taught in all ecclesiastical instruction by the disciples of blessed Pope Gregory in Kent; wishing him to be ordained bishop in Rome, so that he would have a bishop of his own people and language, and thus more perfectly could instruct his subjects in faith or mysteries; as this would not be through an interpreter, but through the language and hand of a man of kin and fellow countryman. This Vighard, coming to Rome with all who had come with him, died of a sickness before receiving the rank of pontiff. But the apostolic pope, lest the legates fulfilling their mission should lack the religious fruits of the faithful, after deliberation, chose one of his own to send as archbishop to Britain, namely Theodore, a man endowed with both secular and ecclesiastical philosophy, and in both languages, Greek and Latin, giving him a colleague and advisor, a man equally vigorous and wise, Abbot Adrian; and because he foresaw that the venerable Benedict would be a wise, industrious, religious, and noble man, he entrusted him with all his bishops, and commanded that, having left the pilgrimage he had undertaken for Christ, he should return to his homeland with a view to greater convenience and bring him a teacher of the truth whom he had diligently sought, who could serve as both interpreter and guide whether he was going there or teaching there. He did as he commanded: they came to Kent, were received very gladly; Theodore ascended to the see of the episcopate; Benedict received the monastery of the blessed apostle Peter to govern; of which the aforementioned Adrian later became abbot.

After governing the monastery for two years, he set out on a journey from Britain to Rome, completing it with the usual success in the third year. He brought back many books of divine learning, either purchased at a fair price or generously given by friends. On his return, when he arrived at Vienna, he retrieved those he had entrusted to friends. Upon entering Britain, he thought to confer with the king of the West Saxons named Coinvalch, with whom he had previously enjoyed friendship and assistance. However, at that very time, he was taken away by an untimely death, and finally turned his feet toward his homeland, the people, and the place where he was born. He approached Ecgfrid, the king of the Transhumbrana region, recounting all that he had done since he left his homeland as a youth; he did not conceal the desire he had for religion, nor what he had learned about ecclesiastical and monastic institutions in Rome and elsewhere, how many divine volumes he had brought back, and how many relics of the blessed apostles or martyrs of Christ he had obtained. He found such favor and familiarity with the king that he immediately granted him land for seventy families and ordered a monastery to be built there for the first pastor of the Church. This was done, as I mentioned in the preface, at the mouth of the River Viri in the North, in the year 674 after the Incarnation of the Lord, in the second indiction, and in the fourth year of King Ecgfrid's reign.

And no more than a year after the monastery was founded, Benedict, having crossed the ocean, sought out Gaul, requesting masons to build him a stone church according to the custom of the Romans, which he had always loved. He received them and brought them back. He showed such diligence in working out of love for blessed Peter, in whose honor he was building, that within a year from the laying of the foundations, you could see the solemn masses being celebrated there with the roofs placed on. As the work approached completion, he sent legates to Gaul to bring glaziers, namely craftsmen from Britain who were previously unknown, to make the windows of the church and its porticoes and dormitories. This was done, and they came; not only did they complete the requested work, but they also enabled the Angles to know and learn such a craft: a craft suitable for either the lamps of the church cloisters or for various uses of vessels. Moreover, the religious buyer took care to import from overseas regions all that pertained to the altar and the ministry of the church, holy vessels, or vestments, since he could not find them at home.

And so that he could also bring ornaments or furnishings from the Roman borders of his church, after establishing the monastery according to the rule, he returned from the fourth journey, laden with more spiritual goods than before. First, he brought back an innumerable supply of books of all kinds; second, he brought a rich abundance of relics of the blessed apostles and martyrs of Christ, which would be beneficial to many English churches; third, he imparted the order of singing, psalming, and ministering in the Church according to the custom of Roman institutions to his monastery, having requested and received from Pope Agatho the archcantor of the church of the blessed apostle Peter and John, the abbot of the monastery of Saint Martin, who would be the future master of the monastery in Britain and would bring Roman customs to the English. Upon arriving there, he not only taught the ecclesiastical knowledge he had learned in Rome to those who were studying but also left behind many written instructions, which are still kept in the library of that same monastery for the sake of memory. Fourth, Benedict brought a valuable gift, a letter of privilege from the venerable Pope Agatho, received with the permission, consent, desire, and encouragement of King Ecgfrid, by which the monastery he built would be perpetually safe and free from all external incursions. Fifth, he brought pictures of holy images to adorn the church of the blessed apostle Peter that he had constructed; namely, an image of the blessed Mother of God, ever-virgin Mary, along with the twelve apostles, which would encircle the apex of the church's dome, spanning from wall to wall; images of the gospel history to decorate the southern wall of the church; images of the visions of the Apocalypse of blessed John to adorn the northern wall, so that all who entered the church, even those unlettered, might behold the always lovable aspect of Christ and his saints, even if in image; or they might recall the grace of the Lord's incarnation with a more vigilant mind; or they might remember to examine themselves more strictly, as if having before their eyes the final judgment.

Therefore, by the virtue, diligence, and piety of the venerable Benedict, King Ecgfrith was greatly pleased and sought to increase the land he had granted to him for the construction of a monastery, as he saw that he had given well and fruitfully, with the possession of forty families. After a year, sending nearly seventeen monks, along with the appointed abbot and priest Ceolfrid, Benedict, at the counsel and even at the command of the aforementioned King Ecgfrith, built the monastery of Saint Paul the Apostle, with the sole purpose that the peace and harmony of both places should be preserved in the same perpetual familiarity and grace; so that just as, for example, the body cannot be separated from the head through which it breathes, the head of the body cannot forget it without which it cannot live, likewise no one would attempt to disturb these monasteries united by the fraternal society of the first apostles. Ceolfrid, whom Benedict appointed as abbot, had been a most diligent assistant to him from the very beginning of the monastery's establishment, and at the appropriate time had gone to Rome for the purpose of learning and worshiping. At that time, he also chose the priest Easterwine from the monastery of Saint Peter as abbot, appointing him to govern the same monastery, so that he could bear the burden he could not carry alone, with the assistance of his beloved fellow soldier's strength. Nor does it seem unreasonable for anyone to have had two abbots for one monastery. This was done frequently for the benefit of the monastery, with Ceolfrid often crossing the ocean, uncertain in his return. For it is also recorded in history that the most blessed Apostle Peter established two pontiffs in Rome to govern the Church due to pressing necessity. And the great abbot Benedict, as the blessed Pope Gregory writes about him, appointed twelve abbots from among his disciples, as he judged it useful, without detriment to charity, but rather for the increase of charity.

Therefore, the aforementioned man took on the care of governing the monastery in the ninth year since it was founded. He remained in it until his death for four years, a noble man, but his nobility was not a matter for boasting, as some do, looking down on others, but directed towards a greater nobility of spirit, as befits a servant of God. He was indeed a cousin of his abbot Benedict, but the genius of both minds was such that the contempt for worldly nobility was of no account, so that neither did he enter the monastery seeking honor for himself above others on account of kinship or nobility, nor did Benedict think it should be offered, but he boasted of keeping the rule in every way on equal terms with his brothers. Indeed, when he had been a minister of King Ecgfrith, having once left behind secular affairs and laid aside arms, taking on spiritual warfare, he remained so humble and most similar to the other brothers that he delighted in being engaged in all the works of the monastery, whether it was to ventilate and thresh, to milk the ewes and calves, in the mill, in the garden, in the kitchen, and in all the monastery's labors, joyful and obedient. Yet even having taken on the governance and rank of abbot, he remained with the same spirit towards all, according to what a certain wise man advises, saying: "They have made you a ruler, do not be exalted, but be among them as one of them, gentle, affable, and kind to all." And indeed, wherever he found it appropriate, he would correct those who sinned against the regular discipline, but more so, diligent in admonishing them with a natural habit of love, so that no one who wished to sin could hide his own restlessness under the clear light of his countenance. Often, for the sake of caring for the monastery's affairs, when he would go off somewhere, wherever he found working brothers, he would immediately join them in work, whether guiding the plow's course, taming iron with a hammer, shaking the fan by hand, or doing some other such task. For he was a strong young man in strength, and sweet in speech; but also cheerful in spirit, generous in giving, and honorable in appearance. He ate the same food as the other brothers, and always shared the same meal in the house, and even before he was abbot, he slept in the common place, so that even when he was struck by illness and already aware of his death by certain signs, he rested for two more days in the dormitory of the brothers. For the remaining five days until the hour of his departure, he placed himself in a more secluded place; on a certain day, going out and sitting in the open air, he called all the brothers to him and, in a manner of natural mercy, gave them a kiss of peace as they wept and mourned for the departure of such a Father and shepherd. He died on the Nones of March, at night, while the brothers were engaged in morning psalmody. He was twenty-four years old when he sought the monastery, lived in it for twelve years, served as a priest for seven years, four of which he governed the monastery; and thus leaving behind earthly limbs and dying members, he sought the heavenly kingdoms.

However, having briefly introduced the life of the venerable Eastervinus, let us return to the order of narration. Having established that abbot Benedict at the monastery of Saint Peter the Apostle, and Ceolfrid at the monastery of Saint Paul, not long after, for the fifth time, he ran from Britain to Rome, enriched as always with countless ecclesiastical gifts, he returned, indeed, with a great supply of sacred volumes, but not less, as before, endowed with the gift of holy images. For at that time he brought pictures of the history of the Lord, with which he crowned the entire church of the blessed Mother of God that he had made in the greater monastery; he also presented images to adorn the monastery and the church of Saint Paul the Apostle, composed with the highest reason from the concordance of the Old and New Testaments: for example, he joined in painting Isaac carrying the wood for his sacrifice and the Lord carrying the cross on which he would suffer, placed next to each other. Likewise, he compared the serpent exalted in the desert by Moses with the Son of Man exalted on the cross. Among other things, he also brought two silken cloaks of incomparable workmanship, which later he exchanged with King Aldfrid and his councilors, for he found Ecgfrid already slain upon his return, and he purchased the land of three families to the south of the River Wear, near the mouth.

But among the joyful things he brought back, he found sad tidings at home: namely, the venerable presbyter Eastervinus, whom he had appointed as abbot before leaving, and a considerable number of the brethren entrusted to him, had already passed from this world due to the pestilence that was raging everywhere. But there was also solace, for in the place of Eastervinus, he learned that a man equally reverend and gentle from the same monastery, namely Sigfrid, a deacon, had been soon appointed by the election of his brethren and his co-abot Ceolfrid; a man sufficiently instructed in the knowledge of the Scriptures, adorned with the best morals, endowed with the marvelous virtue of abstinence, but greatly weakened in the guardianship of virtues by bodily infirmity, laboring to maintain the innocence of his heart due to a harmful and incurable lung ailment.

Not long after, Benedict himself began to be worn down by an increasing illness. In order to prove such an urgency of religion, even the virtue of patience was joined, divine mercy prostrated both in temporal sickness upon the bed, so that after the illness defeated by death, he might be refreshed in the perpetual quiet of heavenly peace and light. For Sigfrid, as we said, having been long tormented by inner distress, reached his last day. And Benedict, through a gradually increasing illness over three years, was so dissolved by paralysis that he became almost completely dead in all the lower parts of his body, only able to live without which a man cannot exist, reserved for the office of patience and virtue; he constantly strove to give thanks to the Author in pain, always to be occupied with the praises of God and the exhortations of his brethren. Benedict often addressed the brothers who came to him about confirming the rule he had established: "For you must not think," he said, "that I have brought forth these decrees to you unlearned in heart. Indeed, I learned all these from the ten and seventeen monasteries which I found to be the best during my long journeys, and I entrusted them to you to be healthily observed." He commanded that the library, which he had brought from Rome, most noble and abundant, be diligently kept intact for the necessary instruction of the Church, nor be defiled through negligence, or carelessly scattered. But he also used to repeat this command to them diligently, that no one in the election of an abbot should consider the lineage of descent, and not more the probity of living and teaching to be sought. "And truly," he said, "I say to you, that in comparison of two evils, it is much more tolerable for me that this whole place in which I made the monastery be reduced to eternal solitude, if God should judge it so, than for my carnal brother, whom we know does not walk in the way of truth, to succeed me in the name of abbot in governing it. Therefore, take great care, brethren, always, that you never seek a father according to lineage, nor from outside. But according to what the rule of the great abbot Benedict once prescribed, according to what the decrees of our privilege contain, you should seek in the assembly of your congregation by common counsel, who according to the merit of life and the teaching of wisdom is deemed more suitable and worthy to be perfected for such ministry, and whomever you all, knowing the best by unanimous inquiry of charity, shall choose, let this one be requested by you from the bishop to be confirmed as abbot with the accustomed blessing. For he who, he said, generates carnal sons in a carnal order, must seek carnal heirs for his carnal and earthly inheritance; but he who begets spiritual sons of God with the spiritual seed of the word, all that they do must be spiritual. Among his spiritual children, let him be esteemed greater who is endowed with a more abundant grace of the spirit, just as earthly parents are accustomed to recognize the first born of their offspring as the beginning of their children, and to lead him in sharing their inheritance as preferable to the others."

Nor should it be omitted that the venerable abbot Benedict, to alleviate the often tedious long night, which he spent sleepless due to the burden of infirmity, would command a reader to recite before him either the example of the patience of Job or some other passage from Scripture to console the sick, so that, depressed in the depths, he might be more vigorously uplifted to the heavens. And since he could not rise to pray at all, nor easily lift his voice or tongue to fulfill the usual course of psalmody, the prudent man learned, prompted by the affection of religion, to call some of the brothers to him at each hour of daily or nightly prayer, who would respond with the customary psalms in two choirs, and he himself, as much as he could, would join them in singing, supplementing what he could not do alone with their assistance.

But when both abbots, weary from prolonged infirmity, saw themselves near death and no longer fit to govern the monastery, for such a great weakness of the flesh had affected them that the power of Christ was perfected in them, it happened that one day, wishing to see and speak to each other before they departed from this world, Sigfrid was carried on a stretcher to the room where Benedict lay in his bed, and with both of them placed together by the hands of the ministers, their heads were laid on the same pillow, a tearful spectacle, nor did they have the strength to bring their faces closer together to kiss each other; yet they fulfilled this fraternal duty: Benedict, having initiated the matter with him and with all the brothers in a healthy counsel, called upon Abbot Ceolfrid, whom he had appointed to oversee the monastery of Saint Paul the Apostle, a man, namely, who was related to him not so much by the necessity of the flesh as by the fellowship of virtues; and he appointed him as Father over both monasteries, with all favoring this and judging it useful, considering it prudent in all respects to maintain peace, unity, and concord among the places, if they held one perpetual father and ruler; frequently recalling the example of the Israelite kingdom, which always remained indestructible against foreign nations and endured inviolate, as long as it was governed by the same leaders of their own people; but after the cause of the sins of their predecessors caused them to be torn apart by mutual strife, it perished for a brief time and faltered from its solid foundation. But he also urged them to remember without interruption that evangelical saying, because every kingdom divided against itself will be desolate.

2

Book Two

Therefore, after two months had passed, the venerable and God-beloved abbot Sigfrid, having passed through the fire and water of temporal tribulations, was brought into the refreshment of eternal rest, entering the house of the heavenly kingdom, rendering his vows to the Lord in the holocausts of perpetual praise, which he had promised with diligent distinction of worldly lips: and then, after four additional months, the victor over vices, Benedict, and the illustrious founder of virtues, succumbed to the infirmity of the flesh and reached the end. The cold night fell with wintry blasts: that day soon to be born was the holy day of eternal happiness, serenity, and light. The brothers gathered at the church, keeping vigil with prayers and psalms through the shadows of the night: and they comforted themselves under the weight of their father's departure with the continuous modulation of divine praise. Others did not leave the chamber in which the sick man, with a strong spirit, awaited the passage from death to life. The Gospel was read throughout the night for the alleviation of pain, as had been customary on other nights, by the priest; the sacrament of the body and blood of the Lord was given as viaticum at the hour of departure; and thus that holy soul, having been purified and tested by long whips of happiness, left the furnace of the earthly body and soared freely to the glory of heavenly beatitude. To his most victorious departure, neither unclean spirits could in any way impede or delay it, nor did the psalm that was sung for him at that time bear witness. For the brothers, gathering at the church at the beginning of the night, chanting the psalter in order, had reached the eighty-second psalm, which begins: "God, who is like you?" The entire text resonates with the truth that the enemies of the name of Christ, whether carnal or spiritual, always attempt to destroy and scatter the Church of Christ and every faithful soul; but on the contrary, they themselves, confused and troubled, shall perish forever, the Lord weakening them, to whom no one is like, who is alone the Most High over all the earth. Hence, it was rightly understood that it was divinely arranged that such a psalm should be sung at the hour when the soul departed from the body, against which no enemy could prevail with the help of the Lord. Sixteen years after he founded the monastery, he rested in the Lord on the day before the Ides of January, buried in the church of blessed apostle Peter; so that he, who while living in the flesh always loved him, through whose opening the door to the heavenly kingdom he entered, would not be long absent from this altar and relics after death. Sixteen, as we said, years the monastery: he governed the first eight by himself without the assumption of another abbot; the remaining eight with venerable and holy men Eastervin, Sigfrid, and Ceolfrid, aiding him in name, authority, and office; the first for four years, the second for three, the third for one. He, too, the third, namely Ceolfrid, a diligent man in all things, sharp in intellect, active in deed, mature in spirit, fervent in zeal for religion, previously, as we have mentioned above, at the command and with the help of Benedict, founded, completed, and governed the monastery of blessed apostle Paul for seven years; and then, for both monasteries, or as we can more rightly say, for the one monastery of the blessed apostles Peter and Paul located in two places, he presided over with diligent governance for twenty-eight years; and all that his predecessor began with excellent works of virtue, he took care to complete no less diligently. Indeed, among other necessary matters of the monastery that he discovered needed to be arranged over a long time of governance, he also built more oratories; he enlarged the vessels and vestments of the altar and church of every kind; he doubled the library of both monasteries, which abbot Benedict had begun with great urgency, with no lesser industry: so that he himself added three volumes of the new translation to one of the old translation that he had brought from Rome; of which one the old man took with him as a gift when returning to Rome, leaving two to each monastery: he also acquired a remarkable work of cosmographers, which Benedict had purchased in Rome, and he bought the land of eight families near the river Fresca from King Aldfrid, a most learned man in Scriptures, for the possession of the monastery of blessed apostle Paul; the arrangement for acquiring this land Benedict had previously established with the same King Aldfrid while he was still alive, but he died before he could complete it. However, for this land later, under the reign of Osred, Ceolfrid, adding a worthy price, received the land of twenty families in a place that in the language of the inhabitants is called the village of Sambuce, because this seemed closer to the same monastery. Sending monks to Rome during the time of the remembrance of Pope Sergius, he received a privilege from him for the protection of his monastery similar to that which Pope Agatho had given to Benedict; which, having been brought to Britain, was confirmed before a synod in the presence of the bishops and the illustrious King Aldfrid. It is not hidden that previously this had been publicly confirmed by the king and bishops of his time in a synod. During his time, he entrusted himself to the monastery of blessed apostle Peter, which was governed by Witmer, an old and religious man, learned in all secular and scriptural knowledge, who donated to the same monastery the land of ten families that he had received in possession from King Aldfrid in the place of the village which is called Daldun, by the right of perpetual possession.

At which point Ceolfridus, after a long discipline of regular observance which he himself, along with his father Benedict, prudently contributed from the authority of the predecessors; after incomparable diligence in praying and singing, by which he did not cease to be exercised daily; after a remarkable fervor in restraining the wicked and a modesty in consoling the sick; after an unusual frugality in food and drink for the rulers, and the humility of his habit; saw himself now older and full of days, no longer able to prescribe the due form of spiritual exercise to his subjects either by teaching or living due to the impediment of old age; pondering many things for a long time in his mind, he decided more usefully, having given the brothers a command, that according to his statutes of privilege and according to the rule of the holy abbot Benedict, they should choose for themselves a father who was more suitable, he himself having been with Benedict in the place of the blessed apostles when he was young: so that he, having been freed from worldly cares for some time before death, might more freely devote himself to quiet secrets; and they, having taken a younger abbot, might more perfectly observe the institutions of regular life according to the age of the master.

Although all resisted at first, and bending their knees with frequent supplications fell into tears and sobs, what he wished was done. And so great was the desire to set out that on the third day after he revealed to the brothers the secret of his intention, he took to the journey. For he feared that what happened might occur, that he might die before he could reach Rome; at the same time avoiding that he might be delayed by friends or honorable men, by whom he was greatly esteemed, and that money might be given to him by some, to whom he could not repay at the time; always having this custom, that if anyone offered him a gift, he would repay it with not lesser grace either immediately or after an appropriate interval. Therefore, after the Mass was sung early in the morning in the church of the blessed Mother of God, always a virgin, Mary, and in the church of the apostle Peter on the day before the Nones of June, Thursday, and with those present having communicated, he was immediately prepared to go. All gathered in the church of Saint Peter, he, having incense burned and having said a prayer at the altar, gives peace to all, standing on the steps, having the censer in hand: hence, with the weeping of all resounding among the litanies, they go out; they enter the oratory of the blessed martyr Lawrence, which was near the dormitory of the brothers; saying farewell for the last time, he admonishes them about preserving mutual love and correcting those who have sinned according to the Gospel; offers grace of his remission and reconciliation to all, if perchance they had sinned; he beseeches all to pray for him, to be at peace with him, if there were any whom he had rebuked more harshly than was just. They come to the shore; again, after giving the kiss of peace to all amid tears, they kneel; he gives a prayer, ascends the ship with his companions. The deacons of the Church ascend with burning candles and carrying a golden cross, he crosses the river, adores the cross, mounts a horse, and departs, leaving behind in their monasteries nearly six hundred brothers.

However, with him gone with his companions, the brothers return to the church, commending themselves and their own to the Lord with tears and prayer: and after a short interval, having completed the psalmody of the third hour, they gather again; they consult about what should be done; deciding to seek the Father from God more quickly by praying, singing, and fasting; they disclose to the monks of blessed Paul, their brothers, through some of those present, as well as some of their own, what they have decided. They agree, and the spirit of both becomes one, all hearts are lifted up, all voices are raised to the Lord. Finally, on the third day, on the Sunday of Pentecost, all who were in the monastery of Saint Peter convene in council, and not a few from the monastery of blessed Paul are present. There is one accord, the same sentiment from both. Therefore, Abbot Huaetberctus is chosen, who from the earliest days of his youth had been instructed not only in the discipline of regular observance in the same monastery but also had been exercised in no small measure in writing, singing, reading, and teaching. He also, coming to Rome during the time of the blessed memory of Pope Sergius, and having stayed there for no small space of time, learned what he judged necessary for himself, wrote down, and reported; moreover, he had served in the office of priest twelve years before this. Therefore, this elected abbot by all the brothers of both aforementioned monasteries, immediately taking some brothers with him, came to Abbot Ceolfrid, waiting for the course of the ship to cross the Ocean: they announce to him whom they have chosen as abbot: "Thanks be to God," he replied, confirming the election, and he received the letter of commendation to be carried to Pope Gregory, for whose memory's sake, we thought it fitting to include a few verses in this work.

"To the Lord in the Lord of lords, most beloved and thrice blessed Pope Gregory, Huaetberctus, your humble servant, abbot of the most blessed monastery of the chief apostles Peter in Saxony, perpetual greetings in the Lord. I do not cease to give thanks for the dispensation of the heavenly examination, together with the holy brothers who desire to bear the sweetest yoke of Christ in these places to find rest for their souls, which you have deemed worthy to appoint as a glorious vessel of election for the governance of the whole Church in our times, so that through this you might fulfill the light of truth and faith, and also sprinkle even the lesser ones sufficiently with the dew of your piety. Moreover, we commend to your holy kindness, most beloved in Christ father and lord, the venerable remains of our most beloved father Ceolfrid, abbot, and our spiritual nurturer and guardian in monastic quietude, liberty, and peace. And first of all, we give thanks to the holy and undivided Trinity, that he, although he departed from us not without our greatest sorrow, groaning, mourning, and the pursuit of tears, nevertheless reached the joys of his long-desired rest: while recalling those things which he had approached, seen, and always adored as a youth, even weary with old age, he devotedly returned to the thresholds of the blessed apostles. And after more than forty long years of labors and continuous cares, in which he presided over the monasteries by the right of an abbot, with an incomparable love of virtue, as if recently summoned to the conversation of heavenly life, having reached the end of his days, and now near death, he again begins to wander for Christ, so that more freely the thorns of ancient secular anxieties might be consumed by the fervent fire of spiritual compunction. Then we also beseech your Paternity, that what we have not merited to do for him, you might fulfill with the diligent gift of utmost piety: knowing for certain that although you have his body, yet we and you have a great intercessor and patron before the heavenly mercy for our transgressions, whether his spirit remains in the body or is released from the bonds of flesh." And the rest, which the following letters contain.

However, upon Huaetberct returning home, Bishop Acca is called and confirms him with the usual blessing into the office of abbot. Among the countless rights of the monastery that he, with keen youthful ingenuity, recovered, he made this especially delightful and pleasing to all: he removed the bones of Abbot Easterwine, which had been placed in the portico of the entrance to the church of the blessed apostle Peter; likewise, the bones of Abbot Sigfrid and his former master, which had been buried outside the sanctuary to the south, and enclosing both in one reliquary but divided by a middle wall, he arranged them within the same church next to the body of the blessed Father Benedict. He did this on the birthday of Sigfrid, that is, the eleventh of the Kalends of September, on which day it also happened by the wonderful providence of God that the venerable servant of Christ, Witmer, whom we mentioned above, departed, and in the place where the aforementioned abbots had previously been buried, he who had been their imitator was interred.

But the servant of Christ, Ceolfrid, as mentioned above, tending to the thresholds of the blessed apostles, before he arrived there, was struck by illness and closed his last day. Arriving at Lingones around the third hour of the day, he departed to the Lord at the tenth hour of that day, and the next day he was honorably buried in the church of the blessed martyrs Geminus, not only by the English in number more than eighty who had been in his company, but also by the inhabitants of that place, for the delayed desire of such a revered elder, dissolved in tears and mourning. For hardly could anyone hold back tears, seeing his companions, some having lost their father, begin their journey; some, having changed their intention of going to Rome, return home to report that he had been buried; and some remain at the tomb of the deceased among those whose language they did not even know, for the extinguishable affection of the Father.

He was seventy-four years old when he died, having served in the priesthood for forty-seven years, ministering in the office of abbot for thirty-five years, or rather forty-three years, because from the very first time when Benedict began to establish his monastery in honor of the most blessed prince of the apostles, he was an individual companion, cooperator, and teacher of regular and monastic institution. And so that the occasion might never diminish the ancient rigor of his custom, whether of age, infirmity, or journey; from the day he departed from his monastery until the day he died, that is, from the day before the Nones of June until the seventh of the Kalends of October, for one hundred fourteen days, except for the canonical hours of prayer, he made it his duty to chant the Psalter twice daily in order; even when he reached the point through illness that he was unable to ride, he was carried on a litter, and daily offered the sacrifice of the saving host to God, except for one day when he was sailing across the Ocean, and three days before his departure.

He died on the seventh of the Kalends of October in the year of our Lord's incarnation 716, on a Friday, after the ninth hour, in the meadows of the aforementioned city: he was buried the next day to the south of the same city, a mile away, in the monastery of the Gemini, with a not small army of those who had come with him, both Angles and the inhabitants of that same monastery or city, resonating psalms. The Gemini martyrs, in whose monastery and church he was established, are Speusippus, Eleusippus, Meleusippus, who were born of one mother in one birth, reborn in the same faith of the Church, together with their grandmother Leonilla, leaving a worthy memory of their martyrdom, who may also grant us unworthy ones and our parent the help of their intercession and protection."

3

Latin Text

LIBER PRIMUS. Religiosus Christi famulus Biscopus cognomento Benedictus, aspirante superna gratia, monasterium construxit in honorem beatissimi apostolorum principis Petri, juxta ostium fluminis Wiri ad Aquilonem, juvante se ac terram tribuente venerabili ac piissimo gentis illius rege Ecgfrido; idemque monasterium annis sedecim, inter innumeros vel itinerum vel infirmitatum labores, eadem qua construxit religione sedulus rexit. Qui, ut beati papae Gregorii verbis, quibus cognominis ejus abbatis vitam glorificat, utar: Fuit vir vitae venerabilis, gratia Benedictus et nomine, ab ipso pueritiae suae tempore cor gerens senile, aetatem quippe moribus transiens, nulli animum voluptati dedit. Nobili quidem stirpe gentis Anglorum progenitus, sed non minori nobilitate mentis ad promerenda semper angelorum consortia suspensus. Denique cum esset minister Osvii Regis et possessionem terrae suo gradui competentem illo donante perciperet, annos natus circiter viginti et quinque fastidivit possessionem caducam, ut acquirere posset aeternam; despexit militiam cum corruptibili donativo terrestrem, ut vero Regi militaret, regnum in superna civitate mereretur habere perpetuum; reliquit domum, cognatos et patriam propter Christum et propter Evangelium, ut centuplum acciperet, et vitam aeternam possideret; respuit nuptiis servire carnalibus, ut sequi valeret Agnum virginitatis gloria candidum in regnis coelestibus; abnuit liberos carne procreare mortales, praedestinatus a Christo ad educandos ei spirituali doctrina filios coelesti in vita perennes.

Dimissa ergo patria Romam adiit, beatorum apostolorum quorum desiderio semper ardere consueverat, etiam loca corporum corporaliter visere atque adorare curavit. Ad patriam mox reversus, studiosius ea quae vidit ecclesiasticae vitae instituta, diligere, venerari, et quibus potuit praedicare non desiit. Quo tempore Alchfridus, supradicti regis Osvii filius, et ipse propter adoranda apostolorum limina Romam venire disponens, comitem eum ejusdem itineris accepit. Quem cum pater suus ab intentione memorati itineris revocaret, atque in patria ac regno suo faceret residere, nihilominus ipse ut bonae indolis adolescens, coeptum confestim explens iter, summa sub festinatione Romam rediit, tempore cujus supra beatae memoriae Vitaliani papae; et non pauca scientiae salutaris quemadmodum et prius hausta dulcedine, post menses aliquot inde digrediens ad insulam Lirinensem, ibidem se monachorum coetui tradidit, tonsuram accepit, et disciplinam regularem monachi voto insignitus debita cum sollicitudine servavit; ubi per biennium idonea monasticae conversationis doctrina institutus, rursus beati Petri apostolorum principis amore devictus, sacratam ejus corpore civitatem repedare statuit.

Nec post longum adveniente nave mercatoria, desiderio satisfecit. Eo autem tempore miserat Ecgberctus Cantuariorum rex de Britannia electum ad episcopatus officium virum nomine Vighardum, qui a Romanis beati Gregorii papae discipulis in Cantia fuerat omni ecclesiastica institutione sufficienter edoctus; cupiens eum sibi Romae ordinari episcopum, quatenus suae gentis et linguae habens antistitem, tanto perfectius cum subjectis sibi populis vel verbis imbueretur fidei vel mysteriis; quanto haec non per interpretem, sed per cognati et contribulis viri linguam simul manumque susciperet. Qui videlicet Vighardus Romam veniens, cum cunctis qui secum venere comitibus, antequam gradum pontificatus perciperet, morbo ingruente defunctus est. At vero papa apostolicus, ne legatariis obeuntibus legatio religiosa fidelium fructu competente careret, inito consilio, elegit de suis quem Britannias archiepiscopum mitteret, Theodorum videlicet, saeculari simul et ecclesiastica philosophia praeditum virum, et hoc in utraque lingua, Graeca scilicet, et Latina, dato ei collega et consiliatore viro aeque strenuissimo ac prudentissimo Adriano abbate; et quia venerabilem Benedictum sapientem, industrium, religiosum ac nobilem virum fore conspexit, huic ordinatum cum suis omnibus commendavit episcopum, praecepitque ut relicta peregrinatione quam pro Christo susceperat, commodi altioris intuitu patriam reversus, doctorem ei veritatis quem sedula quaesierat adduceret, cui vel illo pergenti vel ibidem docenti, pariter interpres existere posset et ductor. Fecit ut jusserat: venerunt Cantiam, gratissime sunt suscepti; Theodorus sedem episcopatus conscendit; Benedictus suscepit monasterium beati Petri apostoli ad regendum; cujus postea praefatus Adrianus factus est abbas.

Quod ubi duobus annis monasterium rexit, tertium de Britannia Romam iter arripiens solita prosperitate complevit, librosque omnis divinae eruditionis non paucos vel placito pretio emptos, vel amicorum dono largitos retulit. Rediens autem, ubi Viennam pervenit, emptitios ibi quos apud amicos commendaverat, recepit. At ingressus Britanniam, ad regem Occidentalium Saxonum nomine Coinvalch conferendum putavit, cujus et ante non semel amicitiis usus, et beneficiis erat adjutus. Sed ipso eodem tempore immatura morte praerepto, tandem ad patriam, gentem solumque in quo natus est pedem convertens, Ecgfridum Transhumbranae regionis regem adiit; cuncta quae egisset ex quo patriam adolescens deseruit replicavit; quo religionis desiderio arderet, non celavit; quid ecclesiasticae, quid monachicae institutionis Romae vel circumquaque didicisset, quot divina volumina, quantas beatorum apostolorum sive martyrum Christi reliquias attulisset, patefecit; tantamque apud regem gratiam familiaritatis invenit, ut confestim ei terram septuaginta familiarum de suo largitus, monasterium inibi primo pastori Ecclesiae facere praeciperet. Quod factum est, sicut et in prooemio memini, ad ostium fluminis Viri ad Aquilonem, anno ab Incarnatione Domini sexcentesimo septuagesimo quarto, indictione secunda, anno autem quarto imperii Ecgfridi regis.

Nec plusquam unius anni spatio post fundatum monasterium interjecto, Benedictus Oceano transmisso Gallias petens, caementarios qui lapideam sibi ecclesiam juxta Romanorum quem semper amabat morem facerent, postulavit, accepit, attulit. Et tantum in operando studii prae amore beati Petri, in cujus honorem faciebat, exhibuit, ut intra unius anni circulum ex quo fundamenta sunt jacta, culminibus superpositis, missarum inibi solemnia celebrari videres. Proximante autem ad perfectum opere, misit legatarios Galliam, qui vitri factores, artifices videlicet Britanniis eatenus incognitos, ad cancellandas Ecclesiae porticuumque et coenaculorum ejus fenestras adducerent. Factumque est, et venerunt; nec solum opus postulatum compleverunt, sed et Anglorum ex eo gentem hujusmodi artificium nosse ac discere fecerunt: artificium nimirum vel lampadis ecclesiae claustris vel vasorum multifariis usibus non ignobiliter aptum. Sed et cuncta quae ad altaris et ecclesiae ministerium competebant, vasa sancta, vel vestimenta, quia domi invenire non potuit, de transmarinis regionibus advectare religiosus emptor curabat.

Et ut ea quoque quae nec in Gallia quidem reperiri valebant, Romanis e finibus Ecclesiae suae provisor impiger ornamenta vel munimenta conferret; quarta illo, post compositum juxta regulam monasterium, profectione completa, multipliciore quam prius spiritualium mercium fenore cumulatus rediit. Primo quod innumerabilem librorum omnis generis copiam apportavit; secundo quod reliquiarum beatorum apostolorum martyrumque Christi abundantem gratiam multis Anglorum ecclesiis profuturam advexit; tertio quod ordinem cantandi, psallendi atque in Ecclesia ministrandi juxta morem Romanae institutionis suo monasterio contradidit, postulato videlicet atque accepto ab Agathone papa archicantore ecclesiae beati apostoli Petri et abbate monasterii beati Martini Joanne, quem sui futurum magistrum monasterii Britannias, Romanum Anglis adduceret. Qui illo perveniens, non solum viva voce quae Romae didicit ecclesiastica discentibus tradidit; sed et non pauca etiam litteris mandata reliquit, quae hactenus in ejusdem monasterii bibliotheca memoriae gratia servantur. Quartum, Benedictus non vile munus attulit, epistolam privilegii a venerabili papa Agathone, cum licentia, consensu, desiderio, et hortatu Ecgfridi regis acceptam, qua monasterium quod fecit ab omni prorsus extrinseca irruptione tutum perpetuo redderetur ac liberum. Quintum, picturas imaginum sanctarum quas ad ornandum ecclesiam beati Petri apostoli quam construxerat detulit; imaginem, videlicet, beatae Dei genitricis semperque virginis Mariae, simul et duodecim apostolorum, quibus mediam ejusdem ecclesiae testudinem, ducto a pariete ad parietem tabulato praecingeret; imagines evangelicae historiae quibus Australem ecclesiae parietem decoraret; imagines visionum Apocalypsis beati Joannis, quibus septentrionalem aeque parietem ornaret, quatenus intrantes ecclesiam omnes etiam litterarum ignari, quaquaversum intenderent, vel semper amabilem Christi sanctorumque ejus, quamvis in imagine, contemplarentur aspectum; vel dominicae incarnationis gratiam vigilantiore mente recolerent; vel extremi discrimen examinis, quasi coram oculis habentes, districtius seipsi examinare meminissent.

Igitur venerabilis Benedicti virtute, industria ac religione, rex Ecgfridus non minimum delectatus, terram quam ad construendum monasterium ei donaverat, quia bene se ac fructuose donasse conspexit, quadraginta adhuc familiarum data possessione, augmentare curavit; ubi post annum missis monachis numero ferme decem et septem, et praeposito abbate ac presbytero Ceolfrido, Benedictus consultu imo etiam jussu praefati Ecgfridi regis, monasterium beati Pauli apostoli construxit, ea duntaxat ratione, ut una utriusque loci pax et concordia, eadem perpetua familiaritas conservaretur et gratia; ut sicut, verbi gratia, corpus a capite per quod spirat non potest avelli, caput corporis sine quo non vivit nequit oblivisci, ita nullus haec monasteria primorum apostolorum fraterna societate conjuncta aliquo ab invicem tentaret disturbare conatu. Ceolfridus autem hic, quem abbatem constituit Benedictus, a primis instituti monasterii prioris exordiis adjutor illi per omnia strenuissimus aderat, et cum eo tempore congruo Romam discendi necessaria simul et adorandi gratia adierat. Quo tempore etiam presbyterum Eastervinum de monasterio beati Petri eligens abbatem, eidem monasterio regendi jure praefecit, ut quem solus non poterat laborem, socia dilectissimi commilitonis virtute levius ferret. Nec ab re videatur cuiquam duos unum monasterium simul habuisse abbates. Fecit hoc frequens illius pro monasterii utilitate profectio, creber trans Oceanum egressus incertusque regressus. Nam et beatissimum Petrum apostolum Romae pontifices sub se duos per ordinem ad regendam Ecclesiam constituisse, causa instante necessaria, tradunt historiae. Et ipse magnus abbas Benedictus, sicut de illo beatus papa Gregorius scribit, duodecim abbates suis discipulis, prout utile judicavit, sine charitatis detrimento, imo pro augmento charitatis praefecit.

Suscepit igitur memoratus vir curam monasterii regendi, nono ex quo fundatum est anno. Permansit in eo usque ad obitum suum annis quatuor, vir nobilis, sed insigne nobilitatis non ad jactantiae materiem, ut quidam, despectumque aliorum, sed ad majorem, ut Dei servum decet, animi nobilitatem convertens. Patruelis quippe erat abbatis sui Benedicti, sed amborum tanta mentis ingenuitas, talis mundanae ingenuitatis fuit pro nihilo contemptus, ut neque iste monasterium ingressus, aliquem sibi prae caeteris ob intuitum consanguinitatis aut nobilitatis honorem quaerendum, neque ille putaret offerendum, sed aequali cum fratribus lance boni propositi juvenis gloriabatur se regularem per omnia servare disciplinam. Et quidem cum fuisset minister Ecgfridi regis, relictis semel negotiis saecularibus, depositis armis, assumpta militia spirituali, tantum mansit humilis, fratrumque simillimus aliorum, ut ventilare cum eis et triturare, oves vitulasque mulgere, in pistrino, in horto, in coquina, in cunctis monasterii operibus jucundus et obediens gauderet exerceri. Sed et abbatis regimine graduque assumpto, eodem animo quo prius manebat ad omnes, juxta id quod quidam sapiens admonet dicens: Rectorem te constituerunt, noli extolli, sed esto in illis, quasi unus ex illis, mitis, affabilis, et benignus omnibus. Et quidem, ubi opportunum comperiebat, peccantes regulari disciplina coercens, sed magis tamen ingenita diligendi consuetudine sedulus admonens, ne qui peccare vellet, et limpidissimam vultus ejus lucem nubilo sibi suae inquietudinis abscondere. Saepe pro curandis monasterii negotiis alicubi digrediens, ubi operantes invenit fratres, solebat eis confestim in opere conjungi, vel aratri gressum stiva regendo, vel ferrum malleo domando, vel ventilabrum manu concutiendo, vel aliud quid tale gerendo. Erat enim et viribus fortis juvenis, et lingua suavis; sed et animo hilaris, et beneficio largus, et honestus aspectu. Eodem quo fratres caeteri cibo, semper eadem vescebatur in domo, ipso quo priusquam abbas esset communi dormiebat in loco, adeo ut etiam morbo correptus et obitus sui certis ex signis jam praescius, duos adhuc dies in dormitorio fratrum quiesceret. Nam quinque reliquos usque ad exitus horam dies in secretiori se aede locabat: qua die quadam egrediens, et sub dio residens, accitis ad se fratribus cunctis, more naturae misericordis osculum pacis eis flentibus ac de abscessu tanti Patris et pastoris moerentibus dedit. Obiit autem per Nonas Martias, noctu, fratribus matutinae psalmodiae laude vacantibus. Viginti quatuor annorum erat cum monasterium peteret, duodecim in eo vixit annis, septem presbyteratu functus est annis, quatuor ex eis monasterii regimen agebat; ac sic terrenos artus moribundaque membra relinquens, coelestia regna petivit.

Verum his de vita venerabilis Eastervini breviter praelibatis, redeamus ad ordinem narrandi. Constituto illo abbate Benedictus monasterio beati Petri apostoli, constituto et Ceolfrido monasterio beati Pauli, non multo post temporis spatio quinta vice de Britannia Romam accurrens, innumeris sicut semper ecclesiasticorum donis commodorum locupletatus rediit, magna quidem copia voluminum sacrorum, sed non minori, sicut et prius, sanctarum imaginum munere ditatus. Nam et tunc dominicae historiae picturas quibus totam beatae Dei genitricis, quam in monasterio majore fecerat, ecclesiam in gyro coronaret; imagines quoque ad ornandum monasterium ecclesiamque beati Pauli apostoli de concordia veteris et novi Testamenti summa ratione compositas exhibuit: verbi gratia, Isaac ligna quibus immolaretur portantem, et Dominum crucem in qua pateretur aeque portantem, proxima super invicem regione, pictura conjunxit. Item serpenti in eremo a Moyse exaltato, Filium hominis in cruce exaltatum comparavit. Attulit inter alia et pallia duo holoserica incomparandi operis, quibus postea ab Aldfrido rege ejusque consiliariis, namque Ecgfridum postquam rediit jam interfectum reperit, terram trium familiarum ad Austrum Wiri fluminis, juxta ostium comparavit.

Verum inter laeta quae veniens attulit, tristia domi reperit: venerabilem videlicet presbyterum Eastervinum quem abiturus abbatem constituerat, simul et fratrum ei commissorum catervam non paucam, per cuncta grassante pestilentia, jam migrasse de saeculo. Sed aderat et solamen, quia in loco Eastervini virum aeque reverentissimum ac mitissimum de monasterio eodem, Sigfridum videlicet, diaconum, electione fratrum suorum simul et coabbatis ejus Ceolfridi, mox substitutum cognovit; virum scientia quidem Scripturarum sufficienter instructum, moribus optimis ornatum, mira abstinentiae virtute praeditum, sed ad custodiam virtutum animi, corporis infirmitate non minime depressum, ad conservandam cordis innocentiam nocivo et irremediabili pulmonum vitio laborantem.

Nec multo post etiam Benedictus ipse morbo coepit ingruente fatigari. Ut enim tantam religionis instantiam etiam patientiae virtus adjuncta probaret, divina utrumque pietas temporali aegritudine prostravit in lectum, ut post aegritudinem morte devictam perpetua supernae pacis et lucis quiete refoveret. Nam et Sigfridus, ut diximus, longa interiorum molestia castigatus diem pervenit ad ultimum. Et Benedictus per triennium languore paulatim accrescente tanta paralysi dissolutus est, ut ab omni prorsus inferiorum membrorum factus sit parte praemortuus, superioribus solum sine quorum vita vivere nequit homo, ad officium patientiae virtutemque reservatis; studebat in dolore semper Auctori gratias referre, semper Dei laudibus fraternisve hortatibus vacare. Agebat Benedictus advenientes saepius ad se fratres de custodienda quam statuerat regula firmare: « Neque enim putare habetis, inquit, quod ex meo haec quae vobis statui decreta indoctus corde protulerim. Ex decem quippe et septem monasteriis quae inter longos meae crebrae peregrinationis discursus optima comperi, haec universa didici, et vobis salubriter observanda contradidi. » Bibliothecam quam de Roma nobilissimam copiosissimamque advexerat, ad instructionem Ecclesiae necessariam, sollicite servari integram, nec per incuriam foedari, aut passim dissipari praecepit. Sed et hoc sedulus eisdem solebat iterare mandatum, ne quis in electione abbatis, generis prosapiam, et non magis vivendi docendique probitatem putaret esse quaerendam. « Et vere, inquit, dico vobis, quia in comparatione duorum malorum, tolerabilius mihi multo est totum hunc locum in quo monasterium feci, si sic judicaverit Deus in solitudinem sempiternam redigi, quam ut frater meus carnalis, quem novimus viam veritatis non ingredi, in eo regendo post me abbatis nomine succedat. Ideoque multum cavetote, fratres, semper, ne secundum genus unquam, ne deforis aliunde, vobis patrem quaeratis. Sed juxta quod regula magni quondam abbatis Benedicti, juxta quod privilegii nostri continent decreta, in conventu vestrae congregationis communi consilio perquiratis, qui secundum vitae meritum et sapientiae doctrinam aptior ad tale ministerium perficiendum digniorque probetur, et quemcunque omnes unanimi charitatis inquisitione optimum cognoscentes elegeritis, hunc vobis accito episcopo rogetis abbatem consueta benedictione firmari. Nam qui carnali, inquit, ordine carnales filios generant, carnali necesse est ac terrenae suae haereditati carnales terrenosque quaerant haeredes; at qui spirituales Deo filios spirituali semine verbi procreant, spiritualia oportet sint cuncta quae agunt. Inter spirituales suos liberos eum majorem qui ampliori spiritus gratia sit praeditus aestiment, quomodo terreni parentes quem primum partu fuderint, eum principium liberorum suorum cognoscere, et caeteris in partienda sua haereditate praeferendum ducere solent. »

Neque hoc reticendum, quod venerabilis abbas Benedictus ad temperandum saepe longae noctis taedium, quam prae infirmitatis onere ducebat insomnem, advocato lectore, vel exemplar patientiae Job, vel aliud quid Scripturarum quo consolaretur aegrotus, quo depressus in infimis vivacius ad superna erigeretur, coram se recitari jubebat. Et quia nullatenus ad orandum surgere, non facile ad explendum solitae psalmodiae cursum linguam vocemve poterat levare, didicit vir prudens, affectu religionis dictante, per singulas diurnae sive nocturnae orationis horas aliquos ad se fratrum vocare, quibus psalmos consuetos duobus in choris resonantibus, et ipse cum eis quatenus poterat psallendo, quod per se solum nequiverat, eorum juvamine suppleret.

At ubi uterque abbas lassatus infirmitate diutina, jam se morti vicinum, nec regendo monasterio idoneum fore conspexit, tanta namque eos affecit infirmitas carnis ut perficeretur in eis virtus Christi, ut cum quadam die desiderantibus eis se invicem priusquam de hoc saeculo migrarent videre et alloqui, Sigfridus in feretro deportaretur ad cubiculum ubi Benedictus et ipse suo jacebat in grabato, eisque uno in loco ministrorum manu compositis, caput utriusque in eodem cervicali locaretur, lacrymabili spectaculo, nec tantum habuere virium ut propius posita ora ad osculandum se alterutrum conjungere possent; sed et hoc fraterno compleverunt officio: inito Benedictus cum eo, cumque universis fratribus salubri consilio, acciit abbatem Ceolfridum, quem monasterio beati Pauli apostoli praefecerat, virum videlicet, sibi non tam carnis necessitudine, quam virtutum societate propinquum; et eum utrique monasterio cunctis faventibus, atque hoc utillimum judicantibus, praeposuit Patrem; salubre ratus per omnia ad conservandam pacem, unitatem, concordiamque locorum, si unum perpetuo patrem rectoremque tenerent; commemorans saepius Israelitici regni exemplum, quod inexterminabile semper exteris nationibus, inviolatumque perduravit, quandiu unis iisdemque suae gentis regebatur a ducibus; at postquam praecedentium causa peccatorum inimico ab invicem est certamine diremptum, periit paulisper, et a sua concussum soliditate defecit. Sed et evangelicam illam monebat sine intermissione recolendam esse sententiam, quia omne regnum in seipso divisum desolabitur.

LIBER SECUNDUS. Igitur post haec revolutis mensibus duobus, primo venerabilis ac Deo dilectus abbas Sigfridus, pertransito igne et aqua tribulationum temporalium, inductus est in refrigerium sempiternae quietis, introiit in domum regni coelestis, in holocaustis perpetuae laudationis reddens sua vota Domino, quae sedula labiorum mundorum distinctione promiserat: ac deinde adjunctis aliis mensibus quatuor, vitiorum victor Benedictus et virtutum patrator egregius, victus infirmitate carnis ad extrema pervenit. Nox ruit hibernis algida flatibus: dies illi mox sancta nascitura aeternae felicitatis, serenitatis et lucis. Convenerunt fratres ad ecclesiam, insomnes orationibus et psalmis transigunt umbras noctis: et paternae decessionis pondus continua divinae laudis modulatione solantur. Alii cubiculum in quo aeger, animo robustus egressum mortis et vitae exspectabat ingressum, non deserunt. Evangelium tota nocte pro doloris levamine, quod et aliis noctibus fieri consueverat, a presbytero legitur; dominici corporis et sanguinis sacramentum, hora exitus instante, pro viatico datur; et sic anima illa sancta longis flagellorum felicium excocta atque examinata flammis luteam carnis fornacem deserit, et supernae beatitudinis libera pervolat ad gloriam. Cujus egressui victoriosissimo, neque ab immundis spiritibus aliquatenus impediendo vel retardando, etiam psalmus qui tum pro eo canebatur, testimonium dat. Namque fratres ad ecclesiam principio noctis concurrentes, psalterium ex ordine decantantes, ad octogesimum tunc et secundum cantando pervenerant psalmum, qui habet in capite: Deus, quis similis erit tibi? Cujus totus hoc resonat textus, quod inimici nominis Christi sive carnales sive spirituales, semper Ecclesiam Christi, semper animam quamque fidelem disperdere ac dissipare conentur; sed e contra ipsi confusi et conturbati, sint perituri in saeculum, enervante illos Domino, cui non est quisquam similis, qui est solus altissimus super omnem terram. Unde recte dabatur intelligi coelitus dispensatum, ut talis diceretur psalmus ea hora qua exiret de corpore anima, cui juvante Domino nullus praevalere posset inimicus. Sexto decimo postquam monasterium fundavit anno, quievit in Domino confessor, pridie Iduum Januariarum, sepultus in ecclesia beati apostoli Petri; ut quem degens in carne semper solebat amare, quo pandente januam regni coelestis intrabat, ab hujus reliquiis et altari post mortem nec corpore longius abesset. Sedecim, ut diximus, annos monasterium: rexit primos octo per se sine alterius assumptione abbatis; reliquos totidem viris venerabilibus et sanctis Eastervino, Sigfrido et Ceolfrido abbatis se nomine, auctoritate et officio juvantibus; primo quatuor annos, secundo tres, tertio unum.

Qui et ipse tertius, id est Ceolfridus, industrius per omnia vir, acutus ingenio, actu impiger, maturus animo, religionis zelo fervens, prius, sicut et supra meminimus, jubente pariter et juvante Benedicto, monasterium beati Pauli apostoli septem annis, fundavit, perfecit, rexit; ac deinde utrique monasterio, vel sicut rectius dicere possumus, in duobus locis posito uni monasterio beatorum apostolorum Petri et Pauli, viginti et octo annos solerti regimine praefuit; et cuncta quae suus predecessor egregia virtutum opera coepit, ipse non segnius perficere curavit. Siquidem inter caetera monasterii necessaria quae longo regendi tempore disponenda comperit, etiam plura fecit oratoria; altaris et ecclesiae vasa, vel vestimenta omnis generis ampliavit; bibliothecam utriusque monasterii, quam Benedictus abbas magna coepit instantia, ipse non minori geminavit industria: ita ut tres pandectes novae translationis, ad unum vetustae translationis quem de Roma attulerat, ipse super adjungeret; quorum unum senex Romam rediens secum inter alia pro munere sumpsit, duos utrique monasterio reliquit: dato quoque cosmographorum codice mirandi operis, quem Romae Benedictus emerat, terram octo familiarum juxta fluvium Fresca ab Aldfrido rege in Scripturis doctissimo in possessionem monasterii beati Pauli apostoli comparavit; quem comparandi ordinem ipse, dum adhuc viveret, Benedictus cum eodem rege Aldfrido taxaverat, sed priusquam complere potuisset obiit. Verum pro hac terra postmodum, Osredo regnante, Ceolfridus, addito pretio digno, terram XX familiarum in loco qui incolarum lingua ad villam Sambuce vocatur, quia haec vicinior eidem monasterio videbatur, accepit. Missis Romam monachis tempore recordationis Sergii papae, privilegium ab eo pro tuitione sui monasterii instar illius quod Agatho papa Benedicto dederat, accepit; quod Britannias perlatum, et coram synodo patefactum, praesentium episcoporum simul et magnifici regis Aldfridi subscriptione confirmatum est, quomodo etiam prius illud sui temporis regem et episcopos in synodo publice confirmasse non latet. Temporibus illius tradens se monasterio beati Petri apostoli, quod regebat veteranus ac religiosus, et in omni tam saeculari quam Scripturarum scientia eruditus Christi famulus Witmer, terram decem familiarum quam ab Aldfrido rege in possessionem acceperat in loco villae quae Daldun nuncupatur, eidem monasterio perpetuae possessionis jure donavit.

At ubi Ceolfridus post multam regularis observantiae disciplinam quam sibi ipsi, pariter ac suus Pater Benedictus, providus ex priorum auctoritate contribuit; post incomparabilem orandi psallendique solertiam, qua ipse quotidianus exerceri non desiit; post mirabilem et coercendi improbos fervorem, et modestiam consolandi infirmos; post insolitam rectoribus et escae potusque parcitatem, et habitus vilitatem; vidit se jam senior et plenus dierum non ultra posse subditis ob impedimentum supremae aetatis, debitam spiritualis exercitii vel docendo vel vivendo praecipere formam; multa diu secum mente versans, utilius decrevit, dato fratribus praecepto, ut juxta sui statuta privilegii juxtaque regulam sancti abbatis Benedicti, de suis sibi ipsi Patrem qui aptior esset eligerent, ipse beatorum apostolorum ubi juvenis cum Benedicto fuerat: quatenus et ipse ante mortem aliquandiu saecul curis absolutus, liberius sibimet secreta quiete vacaret; et illi sumpto abbate juveniore, perfectius juxta aetatem magistri quae vitae regularis essent instituta servarent.

Obnitentibus licet primo omnibus, et in lacrymas singultusque genua cum obsecratione crebra flectentibus, factum est quod voluit. Tantaque erat proficiscendi cupido, ut tertia die ex quo fratribus secretum sui propositi aperuit, iter arriperet. Timebat enim quod evenit, ne priusquam Romam pervenire posset, obiret; simul devitans, ne ab amicis sive viris principalibus quibus cunctis erat honorabilis, ejus coepta retardarentur, et ne pecunia daretur illi a quibusdam, quibus retribuere pro tempore nequiret; hanc habens semper consuetudinem, ut si quis ei aliquid muneris offerret, hoc illi vel statim vel post intervallum competens, non minore gratia rependeret. Cantata ergo primo mane missa in ecclesia beatae Dei genitricis semperque virginis Mariae et in ecclesia apostoli Petri pridie Nonas Junias, quinta feria, et communicantibus qui aderant, continuo praeparatur ad eundum. Conveniunt omnes in ecclesiam beati Petri, ipse thure incenso et dicta oratione ad altare, pacem dat omnibus, stans in gradibus, thuribulum habens in manu: hinc fletibus universorum inter litanias resonantibus, exeunt; beati Laurentii martyris oratorium, quod in dormitorio fratrum erat obvium, intrant; vale dicens ultimum, de conservanda invicem dilectione, et delinquentibus juxta Evangelium corripiendis, admonet; omnibus, si quid forte deliquissent, gratiam suae remissionis et placationis offert; omnes pro se orare, sibi placatos existere, si sint quos durius justo redarguisset, obsecrat. Veniunt ad littus; rursum osculo pacis inter lacrymas omnibus dato, genua flectunt; dat orationem, ascendit navem cum comitibus. Ascendunt et diacones Ecclesiae cereas ardentes et crucem ferentes auream, transit flumen, adorat crucem, ascendit equum et abiit, relictis in monasteriis suis fratribus numero ferme sexcentis.

Illo autem abeunte cum sociis, redeunt ad ecclesiam fratres, se ac sua Domino fletibus et oratione commendant: et post non grande intervallum, completa horae tertiae psalmodia, rursum conveniunt omnes; quid agendum sit consulunt; orando, psallendo, et jejunando Patrem citius a Deo quaerendum decernunt; monachis beati Pauli, fratribus videlicet suis, per eorum quosdam qui aderant, necnon et suorum aliquos, quod decreverint, pandunt. Assentiunt et illi, fit utrorumque animus unus, omnium corda sursum, omnium levantur voces ad Dominum. Tandem die tertia, veniente Dominico die Pentecostes, conveniunt omnes qui erant in monasterio beati Petri in concilium, adsunt et de monasterio beati Pauli seniorum non pauci. Fit una concordia, eadem utrorumque sententia. Eligitur itaque abbas Huaetberctus, qui a primis pueritiae temporibus eodem in monasterio non solum regularis observantia disciplinae institutus, sed et scribendi, cantandi, legendi ac docendi fuerat non parva exercitatus industria. Romam quoque temporibus beatae memoriae Sergii papae accurrens, et non parvo ibidem temporis spatio demoratus, quaeque sibi necessaria judicabat, didicit, descripsit, retulit; insuper et duodecim ante haec annos presbyteri est functus officio. Hic igitur electus abbas ab omnibus utriusque praefati monasterii fratribus, statim assumptis secum aliquibus fratrum, venit ad abbatem Ceolfridum cursum navis qua Oceanum transiret exspectantem: quem elegerant abbatem nuntiant: Deo gratias, respondit, electionem confirmat, et commendatoriam ab eo epistolam apostolico papae Gregorio deferendam suscepit; cujus memoriae causa, putavimus etiam in hoc opere versus aliquot esse ponendos.

« Domino in Domino dominorum dilectissimo, terque beatissimo papae Graegorio, Huaetberctus humilis servus vester, abbas coenobii beatissimi apostolorum principis Petri in Saxonia, perpetuam in Domino salutem. Gratias agere non cesso dispensationi superni examinis, una cum sanctis fratribus qui mecum in his locis ad inveniendam requiem animabus suis suavissimum Christi jugum portare desiderant, quod te nostris temporibus tam glorificum electionis vas regimini totius Ecclesiae praeficere dignatus est, quatenus per hoc quo ipse impleris lumen veritatis et fidei, etiam minores quosque affatim jubare suae pietatis aspergeret. Commendamus autem tuae sanctae benignitati, dilectissime in Christo pater et domine, venerabiles Patris nostri dilectissimi canos, Ceolfridi videlicet abbatis, ac nutritoris tutorisque nostrae spiritualis in monastica quiete libertatis et pacis. Et primum quidem gratias agimus sanctae et individuae Trinitati, quod ipse, etsi non sine maximo nostro dolore, gemitu, luctu, ac prosecutione lacrymarum a nobis abiit; ad suae tamen diu desideratae quietis gaudia sancta pervenit: dum ea quae juvenem se adiisse, vidisse atque adorasse semper recordans exsultabat, etiam senio defessus, beatorum apostolorum devotus limina repetiit. Et post longos amplius XL annorum labores curasque continuas, quibus monasteriis regendis abbatis jure praefuit, incomparabili virtutis amore quasi nuper ad conversationem vitae coelestis accitus, ultima confectus aetate, et prope jam moriturus, rursus incipit peregrinari pro Christo, quo liberius prisca sollicitudinum saecularium spineta camino spirituali fervens compunctionis ignis absumat. Deinde etiam vestrae Paternitati supplicamus, ut quod nos facere non meruimus, vos erga illum ultimae pietatis seduli munus expleatis: pro certo scientes quia etsi vos corpus habetis ipsius, et nos tamen et vos Deo devotum ejus spiritum sive in corpore manentem, sive carneis vinculis absolutum, magnum pro nostris excessibus apud supernam pietatem intercessorem habemus et patronum. » Et caetera, quae epistolae sequentia continent.

Reverso autem domum Huaetbercto, advocatur episcopus Acca, et solita illum in abbatis officium benedictione confirmat. Qui inter innumera monasterii jura quae juvenili sagax solertia recuperabat, hoc inprimis omnibus delectabile et gratificum fecit: sustulit ossa Eastervini abbatis, quae in porticu ingressus ecclesiae beati apostoli Petri erant posita; necnon et ossa Sigfridi abbatis ac magistri quondam sui, quae foris sacrarium ad meridiem fuerant condita, et utraque in una theca sed medio pariete divisa recludens, intus in eadem ecclesia juxta corpus beati Patris Benedicti composuit. Fecit autem haec die natalis Sigfridi, id est, undecimo Kalendarum Septembrium, quo etiam die contigit mira Dei providentia, ut venerandus Christi famulus Witmer, cujus supra meminimus, excederet, et in loco ubi praedicti abbates prius sepulti fuerant, ipse qui eorum imitator fuerat, conderetur.

Christi vero famulus Ceolfridus, ut supradictum est, ad limina beatorum apostolorum tendens, priusquam illo pervenisset, tactus infirmitate diem clausit ultimum. Perveniens namque Lingonas circa horam diei tertiam, decima ipsius diei hora migravit ad Dominum, et crastino in ecclesia beatorum Geminorum martyrum honorifice sepultus est, non solum Anglis genere qui plusquam octoginta numero in ejus fuerant comitatu, sed et illius loci accolis pro retardato tam reverendi senis desiderio, in lacrymas luctusque solutis. Neque enim facile quisquam lacrymas tenere potuit, videns comites ipsius partim patre amisso coeptum iter agere; partim mutata intentione qua Romam ire desiderarant, domum magis, qua hunc sepultum nuntiarent, reverti; partim ad tumbam defuncti inter eos quorum nec linguam noverant, pro in exstinguibili Patris affectu residere.

Erat autem quando obiit annorum septuaginta quatuor, presbyterii gradu functus annis quadraginta septem, abbatis officium ministrans annis triginta quinque, vel potius annis quadraginta tribus, quia scilicet a primo tempore quo Benedictus in honore beatissimi apostolorum principis suum coepit condere monasterium, ipse illi comes individuus, cooperator et doctor regularis et monasticae institutionis aderat. Cui ne prisci morem rigoris, vel aetatis, vel infirmitatis, vel itineris unquam minueret occasio; ex die quo de monasterio suo profectus abiit usque ad diem quo defunctus est, id est, a pridie Nonas Junias usque ad septimum Kalendarum Octobrium diem, per dies CXIV, exceptis canonicis orationum horis, quotidie bis Psalterium ex ordine decantare curavit; etiam cum ad hoc per infirmitatem deveniret, ut equitare non valens feretro caballario veheretur, quotidie missa cantata salutaris hostiae Deo munus offerret, excepto uno, quo Oceanum navigabat, et tribus ante exitum diebus.

Obiit autem septimo Kalendarum Octobrium die, anno ab incarnatione Domini septingentesimo sexto decimo, feria sexta, post horam nonam, in pratis memoratae civitatis: sepultus in crastinum ad austrum ejusdem civitatis milliario primo in monasterio Geminorum astante ac psalmos resonante exercitu non parvo tam Anglorum qui cum eo advenerant, quam monasterii ejusdem vel civitatis incolarum. Sunt autem Gemini martyres in quorum monasterio et ecclesia conditus est, Speusippus, Eleusippus, Meleusippus, qui uno partu matris editi, eadem Ecclesiae fide renati, simul cum avia sua Leonilla, dignam loco illi sui martyrii reliquere memoriam, qui piam etiam nobis indignis et nostro parenti opem suae intercessionis et protectionis impendant.

This work was produced in association with:

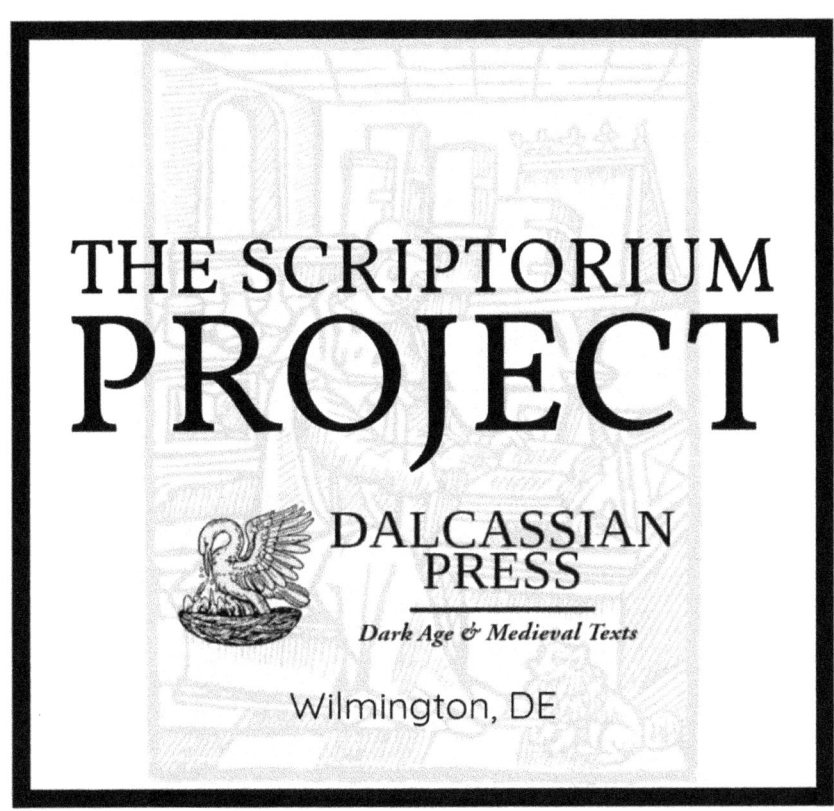

www.ingramcontent.com/pod-product-compliance
Lightning Source LLC
LaVergne TN
LVHW061049070526
838201LV00074B/5234